SCIENTOLOGY
Making the World a Better Pl

M000087823

Founded and developed by L. Ron Hubbard, Scientology is an applied religious philosophy which offers an exact route through which anyone can regain the truth and simplicity of his spiritual self.

Scientology consists of specific axioms that define the underlying causes and principles of existence and a vast area of observations in the humanities, a philosophic body that literally applies to the entirety of life.

This broad body of knowledge resulted in two applications of the subject: first, a technology for man to increase his spiritual awareness and attain the freedom sought by many great philosophic teachings; and, second, a great number of fundamental principles men can use to improve their lives. In fact, in this second application, Scientology offers nothing less than practical methods to better *every* aspect of our existence—means to create new ways of life. And from this comes the subject matter you are about to read.

Compiled from the writings of L. Ron Hubbard, the data presented here is but one of the tools which can be found in *The Scientology Handbook*. A comprehensive guide, the handbook contains numerous applications of Scientology which can be used to improve many other areas of life.

In this booklet, the editors have augmented the data with a short introduction, practical exercises and examples of successful application.

Courses to increase your understanding and further materials to broaden your knowledge are available at your nearest Scientology church or mission, listed at the back of this booklet.

Many new phenomena about man and life are described in Scientology, and so you may encounter terms in these pages you are not familiar with. These are described the first time they appear and in the glossary at the back of the booklet.

Scientology is for use. It is a practical philosophy, something one *does*. Using this data, you *can* change conditions.

Millions of people who want to do something about the conditions they see around them have applied this knowledge. They know that life can be improved. And they know that Scientology works.

Use what you read in these pages to help yourself and others and you will too.

CHURCH OF SCIENTOLOGY INTERNATIONAL

How to raise a happy, healthy child is not something most parents are taught. In fact, many just stumble through the entire process, albeit with the best intentions. Consequently, it is all too common to find an unhappy state of affairs in families, with constant friction between parents and children.

It is not a natural state of affairs. In fact, it can be avoided entirely. L. Ron Hubbard developed many methods to bring out the best in a child—and its parents. In this booklet, you will read about some of these methods and discover how to raise a child without breaking his spirit, how to have a child who is willing to contribute to the family, and how to help a child quickly get over the daily upsets and tribulations of life.

Raising children should be a joy. And can be. In fact, it can be one of the most rewarding of all human experiences. The application of Scientology principles to the bringing up of children can ensure that they are happy, loving and productive, and that they become valued members of the societies in which they live.■

How to Live with Children

The main problem with children is how to live with them. The adult is the problem in child raising, not the child. A good, stable adult with love and tolerance in his heart is about the best therapy a child can have.

The main consideration in raising children is the problem of training them without breaking them. You want to raise your child in such a way that you don't have to control him, so that he will be in full possession of himself at all times. Upon that depends his good behavior, his health, his sanity.

Children are not dogs. They can't be trained like dogs are trained. They are not controllable items. They are, and let's not overlook the point, men and women. A *child* is not a special species of animal distinct from man. A child is a man or a woman who has not attained full growth.

Any law which applies to the behavior of men and women applies to children.

How would you like to be pulled and hauled and ordered about and restrained from doing whatever you wanted to do? You'd resent it. The only reason a child "doesn't" resent it is because he's small. You'd half murder somebody who treated you, an adult, with the orders, contradiction and disrespect given to the average child. The child doesn't strike back because he isn't big enough. He gets your floor muddy, interrupts your nap, destroys the peace of the home instead. If he had equality with you in the matter of rights, he'd not ask for this "revenge." This "revenge" is standard child behavior.

Self-determinism is that state of being wherein the individual can or cannot be controlled by his environment according to his own choice. In that state the individual has self-confidence in his control of the material universe and other people.

A child has a right to his self-determinism. You say that if he is not restrained from pulling things down on himself, running into the road, etc., etc., he'll be hurt. What are you as an adult doing to make that child live in rooms or an environment where he *can* be hurt? The fault is yours, not his, if he breaks things.

The sweetness and love of a child is preserved only so long as he can exert his own self-determinism. You interrupt that and to a degree you interrupt his life.

There are only two reasons why a child's right to decide for himself has to be interrupted—the fragility and danger of his environment and *you*. For you work out on him the things that were done to you, regardless of what you think.

There are two courses you can take. Give the child leeway in an environment he can't hurt and which can't badly hurt him and which doesn't greatly restrict his own space and time. And through Scientology services, you can clean up your own aberrations (departures from rational thought or behavior) to a point where your tolerance equals or surpasses his lack of education in how to please you.

When you give a child something, it's *his*. It's not still yours. Clothes, toys, quarters, what he has been given, *must remain under his exclusive control*. So he tears up his shirt, wrecks his bed, breaks his fire engine. It's *none of your business*. How would you like to have somebody give you a Christmas present and then tell you, day after day thereafter, what you are to do with it and even punish you if you failed to care for it the way the donor thinks you should? You'd wreck that donor and ruin that present. You know you would. The child wrecks your nerves when you do it to him. That's revenge. He cries. He pesters you. He breaks your things. He "accidentally" spills his milk. And he wrecks the possession *on purpose* about which he is so often cautioned. Why? Because he is fighting for his own self-determinism, his own right to own and make his weight felt on his environment. This "possession" is another channel by which he can be controlled. So he has to fight the possession and the controller.

Doubtless, some people were so poorly raised they think *control* is the ne plus ultra (highest point) of child raising. If you want to control your child, simply break him into complete apathy and he'll be as obedient as any hypnotized half-wit. If you want to know how to control him, get a book on dog training, name the child Rex and teach him first to "fetch" and then to "sit up" and then to bark for his food. You can train a child that way. Sure you can. But it's your hard luck if he turns out to be a bloodletter (a person who causes bloodshed).

Of course, you'll have a hard time of it. This is a *human being*. It will be tough because man became king of the beasts only because he couldn't as a species be licked. He doesn't easily go into an obedient apathy like dogs do. *Men* own *dogs* because men are self-determined and dogs aren't.

The reason people started to confuse children with dogs and started training children with force lies in the field of psychology. The psychologist worked on "principles" as follows:

"Man is evil."

"Man must be trained into being a social animal."

"Man must adapt to his environment."

As these postulates aren't true, psychology doesn't work. And if you ever saw a wreck, it's the child of a professional psychologist. Attention to the world around us instead of to texts somebody thought up after reading somebody's texts, shows us the fallacy of these postulates.

The actuality is quite opposite the previous beliefs.

The truth lies in this direction:

Man is basically good.

Only by severe aberration can man be made evil. Severe training drives him into nonsociability.

Man must retain his personal ability to adapt his environment to him to remain sane.

A man is as sane and safe as he is self-determined.

In raising your child, you must avoid "training" him into a social animal. Your child begins by being more sociable, more dignified than you are. In a relatively short time the treatment he gets so checks him that he revolts. This revolt can be intensified until he is a terror to have around. He will be noisy, thoughtless, careless of possessions, unclean—anything, in short, which will annoy you. Train him, control him and you'll lose his love. You've lost the child forever that you seek to control and own.

Permit a child to sit on your lap. He'll sit there, contented. Now put your arms around him and constrain him to sit there. Do this even though he wasn't even trying to leave. Instantly, he'll squirm. He'll fight to get away from you. He'll get angry. He'll cry. Recall now, he was happy before you started to hold him.

Your efforts to mold, train, control this child in general react on him exactly like trying to hold him on your lap.

Of course you will have difficulty if this child of yours has already been trained, controlled, ordered about, denied his own possessions. In mid-flight, you change your tactics. You try to give him his freedom. He's so suspicious of you he will have a terrible time trying to adjust. The transition period will be terrible. But at the end of it you'll have a well-ordered, well-trained, social child, thoughtful of you and, very important to you, a child who loves you.

The child who is under constraint, shepherded, handled, controlled, has a very bad anxiety postulated. His parents are survival entities. They mean food, clothing, shelter, affection. This means he wants to be near them. He wants to love them, naturally, being their child.

But on the other hand his parents are nonsurvival entities. *His whole being and life depend upon his rights to use his own decision about his movements and his possessions and his body.* Parents seek to interrupt this out of the mistaken idea that a child is an idiot who won't learn unless "controlled." So he has to fight shy, to fight against, to annoy and harass an enemy.

Here is anxiety. "I love them dearly. I also need them. But they mean an interruption of my ability, my mind, my potential life. What am I going to do

A child needs his parents' support for many aspects of his survival. But if they also severely interrupt his decisions of his life he is given a huge problem which can cause him much worry.

about my parents? I can't live with them. I can't live without them. Oh, dear, oh, dear!" There he sits running this problem through his head. That problem, that anxiety, will be with him for eighteen years, more or less. And it will half wreck his life.

Freedom for the child means freedom for you. Abandoning the possessions of the child to their fate means eventual safety for the child's possessions.

What terrible willpower is demanded of a parent not to give constant streams of directions to a child! What agony to watch his possessions going to ruin! What upset to refuse to order his time and space!

But it has to be done if you want a well, a happy, a careful, a beautiful, an intelligent child!

A Child's Right to Contribute

You have no right to deny your child the right to contribute.

A human being feels able and competent only so long as he is permitted to contribute as much or more than he has contributed to him.

A man can over-contribute and feel secure in an environment. He feels insecure the moment he under-contributes, which is to say, gives less than he receives. If you don't believe this, recall a time when everyone else brought something to the party but you didn't. How did you feel?

A human being will revolt against and distrust any source which contributes to him more than he contributes to it.

Parents, naturally, contribute more to a child than the child contributes back. As soon as the child sees this he becomes unhappy. He seeks to raise his contribution level; failing, he gets angry at the contributing source. He begins to detest his parents. They try to override this revolt by contributing more. The child revolts more. It is a bad dwindling spiral because the end of it is that the child will go into apathy.

You *must* let the child contribute to you. You can't order him to contribute. You can't command him to mow the grass and then think that is contribution. He has to figure out what his contribution is and then give it. If he hasn't selected it, it isn't his, but only more control.

A baby contributes by trying to make you smile. The baby will show off. A little older he will dance for you, bring you sticks, try to repeat your work motions to help you. If you don't accept those smiles, those dances, those sticks, those work motions in the spirit they are given, you have begun to interrupt the child's contribution. Now he will start to get anxious. He will do unthinking and strange things to your possessions in an effort to make them "better" for you. You scold him. That finishes him.

Something else enters in here. And that is *data*. How can a child possibly know what to contribute to you or his family or home *if* he hasn't any idea of the working principles on which it runs?

A family is a group with the common goal of group survival and advancement. The child not allowed to contribute or failing to understand the goals and working principles of family life is cast adrift from the family. He is shown he is not part of the family because he can't contribute. So he becomes antifamily—the first step on the road to being antisocial. He spills milk, annoys your guests and yells outside your window in "play." He'll even get sick just to make you work. He is shown to be nothing by being shown that he isn't powerful enough to contribute.

You can do nothing more than accept the smiles, the dances, the sticks of the very young. But as soon as a child can understand, he should be given the whole story of the family operation.

What is the source of his allowance? How come there is food? Clothes? A clean house? A car?

Daddy works. He expends hours and brains and brawn and for this he gets money. The money, handed over at a store, buys food. A car is cared for because of money scarcity. A calm house and care of Daddy means Daddy works better and that means food and clothes and cars.

Education is necessary because one earns better after he has learned.

Play is necessary in order to give a reason for hard work.

Give him the whole picture. If he's been revolting, he may keep right on revolting. But he'll eventually come around.

First of all a child needs *security*. Part of that security is understanding. Part of it is a code of conduct which is invariable. What is against the law today can't be ignored tomorrow.

You can actually handle a child physically to defend your rights, so long as he owns what he owns and can contribute to you and work for you.

Adults have rights. He ought to know this. A child has as his goal, growing up. If an adult doesn't have more rights, why grow up? Who the devil would be an adult these days anyway?

The child has a duty toward you. He has to be able to take care of you; not an illusion that he is, but actually. And you have to have patience to allow yourself to be cared for sloppily until by sheer experience itself—not by your directions—he learns how to do it well. Care for the child? Nonsense! He's probably got a better grasp of immediate situations than you have, you beaten-up adult. Only when he's almost psychotic with aberration will a child be an accident-prone.

You're well and enjoy life because you aren't *owned*. You *couldn't* enjoy life if you were shepherded and owned. You'd revolt. And if your revolt was quenched, you'd turn into a subversive. That's what you make out of your child when you own, manage and control him.

Potentially, parent, he's saner than you are and the world is a lot brighter. His sense of values and reality are sharper. Don't dull them. And your child will be a fine, tall, successful human being. Own, control, manage and reject and you'll get the treatment you deserve—subversive revolt.

WORKING WITH
A CHILD'S WILLINGNESS

How then, without using force, do you get a child to do things?

If you take an individual and *make* him play a musical instrument (as parents and schools do), his ability to play that instrument will not improve. We would first have to consult with him as to what his ambitions are. He would eventually at least have to agree with the fact that it is a good thing to play an instrument.

Take, for example, a "bad boy." He cannot be put in school and has to be sent to a military school. They are going to force him in order to change him. Occasionally this bad boy is sent to a school which simply thinks the best way to handle such cases is to find something in which he is interested and to allow him to do it. Such a school once existed in California and consecutively produced geniuses. The roster of World War II's scientists practically marched from that particular school. They figured that it must have been the example set by the professor, his purity in not smoking cigars or something like that.

What actually happened was this: They took a boy with whom nobody got any results and said, "Isn't there anything you would like to do?" The boy said "No," and they answered, "Well, fuss around in the lab or grounds or something and someday you may make up your mind." The boy thought this over and decided that he wanted to be a chemist. Nobody ever sent him to a class and told him to crack a book, and nobody ever complained very much when he blew up something in the laboratory, and the next thing you knew the boy was an excellent chemist. Nobody interrupted his desire to be a chemist. It existed then, and from that point on he was not himself interrupting his willingness to be a chemist. Educationally, this is a very interesting point.

Consulting Willingness

People will permit you to take things away from them if you do it gracefully and don't upset their willingness too much. The way you make a greedy or a selfish child is to *make* him, against his will, give up things to other children. You will eventually drive him into the "only-one" category—feeling he is the only person who really matters at all. Parents usually never consult the child's willingness. They consult his havingness, his ability to own or possess, then handle it and they have a spoiled child.

It is interesting to watch a child that has been around somebody who always consulted him but didn't take very good care of him as opposed to a child who had the best of care but who never was consulted.

A little boy is sitting on the floor playing with blocks and balls and is having a good time. Along comes the nurse who picks him up and takes him into the other room and changes his diapers, and he screams bloody murder the whole way. He doesn't like it. She keeps on doing this to him, placing him around, never consulting his power of choice and he will eventually grow up obsessed with the power of choice. He has to have his way. He becomes very didactic—assertive of his own rightness. He is trying to hold down the last rungs of it, and his ability will be correspondingly poor, particularly in the handling of people.

Now, this is quite different. You know the child is hungry, and you know he ought to eat. The child will eat if he is kept on some sort of routine. If supper is served routinely at 6:00, he will get used to eating at 6:00, and his willingness will never quite be overwhelmed. He finds out that food is there at 6:00 and so he makes up his mind to eat at 6:00. You provide the food and he provides the willingness. If you don't override that, he will never have any trouble about food.

Then somebody comes along and talks to him and says, "Wouldn't you like to go into the other room and change your clothes?" and the answer is "No." You are making a horrible mistake if you proceed from that point on the basis of "Well, I'll give you a piece of candy," persuade, seduce, coax, etc. That is psychology, the way psychologists handle situations, and it doesn't really work.

You take one of two courses. Either you use excellent control with lots of communication, or you just let him grow. There is no other choice. Kids don't like to be mauled and pulled around and not consulted. You can talk to a child and if your degree of affection, agreement and communication with him are good, you can make him do all sorts of things. He will touch the floor, his head, point you out and find the table. He will fool around for a while and after that you can just say do so-and-so and "Let's go and eat," and he will do it. He has found out that your commands are not necessarily going to override the totality of his willingness. So your commands are therefore not dangerous. You have confronted him and he can confront you. Therefore you and he can do something.

A child sometimes says "I want to stay up with you" and they insist on doing so, exerting their power of choice. Just letting children do what they are doing and not interfering with them and not exerting any control on them is psychology. They are never going to be in communication with anybody; they won't grow or get experience in life for they didn't change their havingness. They didn't have to change their mind, work, exercise or do anything. But they respond very readily to good control and communication, but it certainly takes good communication to override this—not persuasion but good communication.

People think that persuasion works with children. It doesn't. It's communication that does the trick. You say, "Well, it's time for you to go to bed now," and he says, "No." Don't stay on the subject. Leave it alone and just talk about something else, "What did you do today?" "Where?" "How?" "Oh, did you? Is that a fact?" "Well, how about going to bed?" and the answer will be "Okay."

One doesn't have to use force. Go into communication with the child, and control follows this as an inevitability. Omit control from the beginning when bringing up a child and he who looks to you for a lot of his direction and control is gypped. He thinks you don't care about him.

However, as in the case with the playing of musical instruments, learning of languages or the arts and abilities, consult the child's *willingness*.

ALLOWING CHILDREN TO WORK

The basic difficulty with all juvenile delinquency is the one-time apparently humane program of forbidding children to labor in any way.

Doubtless it was once a fact that child labor was abused, that children were worked too hard, that their growths were stunted and that they were, in general, used. It is highly doubtful if the infamous Mr. Marx ever saw in America young boys being pulled off machines dead from work and thrown onto dump heaps.

Where there was an abuse of this matter, there was a public outcry against it, and legislation was enacted to prevent children from working. This legislation with all the good intention of the world is, however, directly responsible for juvenile delinquency.

Forbidding children to work, and particularly forbidding teenagers to make their own way in the world and earn their own money, creates a family difficulty so that it becomes almost impossible to raise a family, and creates as well, and particularly, a state of mind in the teenager that the world does not want him, and he has already lost his game before he has begun it. Then with something like universal military training staring him in the face so that he dare not start a career, he is of course thrust into a deep subapathy (state of disinterest below apathy) on the subject of work, and when he at length is faced with the necessity of making his own way in the world, he rises into an apathy and does nothing about it at all.

It is highly supportive of this fact that our greatest citizens worked, usually when they were quite young. In the Anglo-American civilization the highest level of endeavor was achieved by boys who, from the age of twelve, on farms, had their own duties and had a definite place in the world.

Children, in the main, are quite willing to work. A two-, three-, four-year-old child is usually found haunting his father or her mother trying to help out either with tools or dust rags; and the kind parent who is really fond of the children responds in the reasonable and long-ago-normal manner of being patient enough to let the child actually assist. A child so permitted then develops the idea that his presence and activity is desired and he quite calmly sets about a career of accomplishment.

The child who is warped or pressed into some career, but is not permitted to assist in those early years, is convinced that he is not wanted, that the world has no part of him. And later on he will come into very definite difficulties regarding work. However, the child who at three or four wants to work in this modern society is discouraged and is actually prevented from working, and after he is made to be idle until seven, eight or nine, is suddenly saddled with certain chores.

Now, this child is already educated into the fact that he must not work and so the idea of work is a sphere where he "knows he does not belong," and so he always feels uncomfortable in performing various activities.

Later on in his teens, he is actively prevented from getting the sort of a job which will permit him to buy the clothes and treats for his friends which he feels are demanded of him, and so he begins to feel he is not a part of the society. Not being part of the society, he is then against the society and desires nothing but destructive activities.

HANDLING A CHILD'S UPSETS AND MISHAPS

This section provides many techniques for a parent or anyone to use to help a child recover rapidly from the bumps, bruises, scrapes, scares and upsets that are often part of growing up.

For the most part, the techniques which follow utilize communication between oneself and the child as their main therapeutic agent. Communication is vitally important in dealing with children, as it is in any aspect of Scientology.

The actions described below all classify as assists. An assist is an action undertaken to help an individual obtain relief from an immediate troublesome difficulty. These assists should be used in addition to those in the "Assists for Illnesses and Injuries" booklet whenever circumstances require. The benefits for the child and the family can be considerable.

Childhood Injuries

There are many things one can do to aid a child who suffers a minor fall, cut or the like. In young children, often just letting them cry out seems to be enough. When a child is hurt, most people find themselves speaking comforting and consoling words almost before they know it. And what they say is usually what they have said a hundred times before when the child was hurt. This can remind the child of the whole chain of earlier injuries.

Parents can help a child most by saying nothing. It may take a short while to train themselves not to speak when the child is hurt, but it is not difficult to form the habit of remaining silent. Silence need not inhibit affection. One may hold the child, if he wants to be held, or put an arm around him. Often, if nothing is said, a young child will cry hard for a minute or so, and then suddenly stop, smile, and run back to what he was doing. Allowing him to cry seems to release the tension resulting from the injury and no assist is needed if this occurs. In fact, it is often very difficult to make the child return to the moment of injury if he has released the tension this way.

"Tell Me About It"

If the child does not spontaneously recover after a moment or two of crying, then wait until he has recovered from the short period of lowered awareness that accompanies an injury. It is usually not difficult to tell when a child is dazed and when he is not. If he still cries after the dazed period, it is usually because other previous injuries have been restimulated (reactivated due to similar circumstances in the present approximating circumstances of the past). In this case, an assist is valuable. On older children (age five and up) an assist is usually necessary.

When the child is no longer dazed, ask him, "What happened? How did you get hurt? Tell me about it."

As he begins to tell about it, switch him to the present tense if he doesn't tell the story in the present tense spontaneously. Try it this way:

"Well—I was standing on a big rock and I slipped and fell, and..." (crying)

"Does it hurt when you are standing on the rock?"

"No."

"What happens when you are standing on the rock?"

"I slip..." (crying)

"Then what happens?"

"I fall on the ground."

"Is there grass on the ground?"

"No—it's all sandy."

"Tell me about it again."

You can take the child through it several times until he gets bored or laughs. There is nothing difficult about it. After a child has had a few assists this way, he will, upon being injured, run to the person who can administer this painless help and reassurance, demanding to "tell about it."

A child who has hurt herself can be markedly assisted by communication.

Getting her to explain what happened can be therapeutic.

Telling it to someone who's interested will dissipate any upset and enable the child to feel better.

Directing a Child's Attention

Many people habitually tell a child, "Don't do that or you'll get sick," "My goodness, you're certainly getting a bad cold," "You'll get sick if you keep on with that," "I just know Johnny's going to get measles if he goes to school," and countless other such pessimistic suggestions. They also use thousands of "Don'ts," "Can'ts," and "Control yourself" phrases. Parents may watch themselves for these phrases, and avoid their use as much as possible. With a little imagination and practice, it is not difficult to find ways of keeping children safe without using constant verbal restraints. As much as possible, suggestions made to a child should be positive. Graphically illustrating what happens to a glass bottle when it drops will get the idea across better than a thousand screams of "Get away from that!" or "Put that down!"

Smooth, gentle motions and a quiet voice will go far toward averting restimulation when children are being handled. Anyone who wishes to work successfully with children will cultivate these attributes. They are particularly valuable in emergencies.

If a child's attention must be obtained quickly because of a potentially dangerous situation developing too far away to enable the guardian to reach the child in a hurry, calling his name loud enough to be heard will do the trick harmlessly. It is much better than screamed injunctions to "Stop!" "Stay there!" "Don't do that!" and so on. It is not nearly so likely to restimulate him.

Remembering

Asking the child to remember may be used in hundreds of situations that arise from day to day: whenever the child is fretful, unhappy and crying over something; when he is feeling slightly sick; when he is obviously restimulated by something; when he has overheard a dramatization (a replay in the present of something that happened in the past) or someone has punished him severely or uncorked a dramatization directed toward him; when he feels rejected—in fact, every time a child is unhappy or nervous for any reason or when you know that he has had a highly restimulative experience.

The principle here is to get at the specific phrases and situations causing the restimulations. Of course this technique can be used only after the child has learned to talk enough to give a coherent account of what he is thinking and feeling.

If the child is feeling upset (not seriously ill) you may begin by asking him when he felt this way before. Usually a child will remember. As you ask further questions about what was happening, what he was doing at the time, who was talking, what was said, how he felt, he will describe the scene graphically. When he does so, simply have him go through it again a few times. When you come to the end say, "Tell me about it again. Where were you when Daddy was talking?" "Tell it again." Or, simply, "Let's see now, you were sitting on the couch when Daddy says—what does he say?" Any simple phrase which will return the child to the beginning of the scene may be used.

There is no need to make this action complex. Children understand "Tell it again." They love to hear stories over and over again, themselves, and they love to tell their stories to an interested audience. But don't be overly sympathetic. Show affection and interest, yes. But don't croon or moan, "Poor baby, poor little thing!" or similar phrases. To do so may tend to prompt the child to consider the injury or upset *valuable* in that it got him special attention and sympathy.

The more you can enter a child's reality, the better you will be able to help him. Imitate his voice tones, his "Yeah!" "You did!" "And then what?"—adapt yourself to his graphic mimicry, widened eyes, breathless interest or whatever his mood and tone may be—but not to the extent of parroting, of course. If you cannot do it well, then just be simple, natural and interested.

Often, when he is restimulated, a child will use one or two phrases over and over again. In that case you can start with, "Who says that?" or "Who's saying that to you?" or "When did you hear that?"

Sometimes he will insist, "I say it, 'Shut up, you old fool!'" or whatever the phrase is. Then ask, "Who else says it?" or "See if you can remember when you heard somebody else say it," and he will usually start telling you about an incident.

When a child experiences something upsetting or traumatic, similar incidents can reactivate in his mind.

These fall away when the child is gotten to talk about the current upset.

The child should be guided into relating what happened as though it were occurring in the present. This will discharge any trauma connected with it.

One woman, working with her daughter, was astounded when the child said, "You said it, Mummy, a long time ago." "Where were you when I said it?" "Oh, I was only a little thing—in your tummy." This probably won't happen often. But as the child gets the idea, it may happen sooner or later. Whatever the incident, just go on with questioning to build up the incident. "What were you doing? Where were you? Where was I? What was Daddy saying? What did it look like? What did you feel like?" and so on. Have the child recall the incident a few times until he laughs. This will release him from the restimulation.

Use of Dolls or Stuffed Animals

If the father knows that the child has overheard a dramatization or has been severely punished or scolded, he may handle this a few hours after the event by asking about it. "Do you remember when I shouted at Mother last night?" If the child is not used to expressing his anger to his parents, or if he has been severely repressed in the past, it may take some coaxing to get him to tell about it. While doing so, try to assure him by your manner that it is perfectly all right for him to talk about it. If he simply cannot, you might try to get him to play it out. If the child plays with dolls or toy animals you may, in play with him, get him to make the dolls or toys act out the dramatization.

"This is the mama doll. And this is the papa doll. What does the mama doll say when she is mad?" Very often this will take the child right into the scene, and if you let him really open up and describe the scene without condemnation, listening in a sympathetic, interested way, and encouraging him with a well-placed, "Yes...and then what?" he will soon drop the pretense and begin to tell you directly what he overheard. Even if he does not do this and, as children often do, he runs over the scene a couple of times with his dolls or toys, it will lessen in intensity to a large extent.

Overhearing an upset or fight between parents can be extremely disturbing.

A parent can help dissipate the child's concern by getting her to use dolls to demonstrate what happened.

The child re-creates the experience with the dolls...

... and any lingering upset on the child's part can quickly fade away.

Drawing Pictures

Instead of dolls or toys, you may have the child draw pictures. "Draw me a picture of a woman and a man.... What are they doing? Draw me a picture of a woman crying," and so on. The emphasis should always be on the adult who was dramatizing, and not on the child who was bad, if that happened. Drawing pictures, playing house with a child: "And then you say...?" "And then I say...?" or simply getting the child to make up a story about it will help.

Anger

With children who have not been inhibited in their expressions of anger against parents, these subterfuges (deceptions) are not usually necessary. They will tell freely and dramatize scenes they overheard or scoldings they got, if you act as an interested audience and encourage them to build up the scene. If you watch children playing, you will often see them doing exactly that, mimicking their parents and other adults in their dramatizations.

Sometimes just asking a child, "What happened to make you feel bad?" or "What did I say to make you feel that way?" will bring out and alleviate the restimulative elements in the present situation.

Everyone is familiar with the violent threats children can think up when they are frustrated: "I'll tear him to pieces and throw him in the river; I'll make them all go in a closet and lock it up and throw away the key and then they'll be sorry," and so on. If you encourage them by "Yes? And then what will you do?" or "Gee, that would be something!" they will keep on for a while and then they often will suddenly pop right out of the upset and go on with what they were doing.

If a child is angry, let him be angry, even if you are the victim. Let him act out his anger, and usually it will disappear quickly. But if you try to suppress it, it will grow worse and last longer. Letting a child react to a frustrating situation without further suppression seems to release the energy of the frustration and will bring him out of it more quickly than almost anything else.

Fear

If a child is in fear, let him tell you about it, giving him all the encouragement you can. This is particularly effective in nightmares. Wake the child, hold him quietly until his crying calms a little, and ask him about the nightmare, taking him through it several times until he is no longer frightened. Then ask him about a pleasant memory, and have him tell you that before leaving him. If he doesn't want to sleep alone after that, do not make him face his fear. Stay with him and encourage him to talk about it until he is no longer afraid, even if this takes some time. In asking about fears, you can use the phrase "the same as." If the child is afraid of the dark, ask him, "What is the same as dark?" If he is afraid of animals, a similar question will cause him to analyze his fear. Perhaps you will not always be successful on the first questioning, but if you continue patiently you'll soon get an answer that will tell you an incident he has his attention on and you can help the child handle this by talking about what occurred.

Grief

If the child is in grief, a good way to begin is, "What are you crying about?" After a child has told what he is crying about a few times, each time being helped by questioning about the incident, and when his crying has abated (become less), you may ask, "What else are you crying about?"

Actually, just letting him cry until he gets out of it will often be enough. This is especially true if you are in close contact with him and he knows he can count on you for support and assistance.

Don't try to stop a child from crying by simply telling him not to cry. Either handle the incident that caused the crying by asking what happened and getting him to tell about it until he is laughing, or let him cry it out while you caress or hold him. No words in this case; just affection.

Irritableness

If the child is simply fretful and "unmanageable," you can often get him out of it by diverting his attention, by introducing a new and fascinating story or picture book or a toy or, in the case of a very young child, something which glitters. This is an old technique, but it is valid. If the child is fretful, the chances are that he is in boredom, which means that the particular activity he was interested in has been suppressed somehow. He is looking for something new but is unable to find it. If you can give him something to interest him, he will become more cheerful quickly. Do not, however, make frantic efforts to attract his attention, plaguing him with jerky movements and such attention diverters as, "See, baby, see the pretty watch!" and if that fails to have an instantaneous effect, jumping to some other object. This will often only confuse him. Move smoothly and quietly, keep your voice soft and calm, and direct his attention to one new thing. That should be enough.

If none of these work, you can sometimes free him from the dramatization by bringing him up to present time with intense physical stimulation, like playful wrestling or some other vigorous exercise.

If you can get the child's attention long enough, you can ask him to tell you about some nice thing that happened. He may do it reluctantly at first, but as you encourage it he will often go right into the pleasurable memory, and pretty soon he will be cheerful again.

Making a new game of remembering provides a constructive and pleasant way to keep a child occupied during long trips, periods of waiting, periods of convalescence, and so on.

Children naturally have a good ability to recall. They love to talk about past moments of pleasure. A good deal of a child's conversation is filled with the wonderful things he has done or hopes to do, and he often talks spontaneously about times where he has been frightened or unhappy.

Teach a child to relate all pleasure moments by asking him what happened when he went to the zoo or went swimming. When he begins to tell you, switch him subtly to present tense, as suggested, if he fails to do so himself. Tell him to feel the water, feel himself moving, see what is going on, hear what people are saying and the sounds around him. This will help build his recall of the various things he perceived. But don't insist on a full account of the perceptions if the child is swiftly and surely recalling the incident, telling about it fluently. It doesn't take much to get a child to do this.

You can introduce the game by saying, "Let's play remembering," or "Tell me about when you went to…" or "Let's pretend we're going to the zoo again," or any other such casual phrase. Enter into the tale as much as you can, adopting the child's tone and manner if you can do it easily, and always being interested and eagerly awaiting the next detail.

Whenever a child comes to tell you about an accident he had or something that frightened him or made him unhappy, listen to it and have him go over it several times. As children learn how to "play remembering" and learn what it does for them, they will begin to ask for this when they want or need it.

There are many more assists that can be used to help children. Consult the end of this booklet to find a book containing these.

Again, the main points in dealing with a child's upsets or injuries are:

1. Give assists for minor injuries, if necessary, or let the child cry it out if that seems to be enough.

2. Get the child to remember the last time it happened or get him to tell you in full what happened that made him unhappy.

3. Teach a child to remember by having him tell you past pleasure moments.

4. Use recall of pleasure moments or other techniques for bringing the child out of moments of upset up to present time.

Such care will keep the child healthier and happier.

HEALTHY BABIES

An incorrectly fed baby is not only unhappy, he is unhealthy, a matter of concern to any new parent. Proper nourishment is, of course, a necessary ingredient to good health. Based on personal experience, here is something that worked; it is being offered as a helpful tip to parents who seek better ways to raise healthy children.

Some hospitals and medicos have adopted, apparently, the slogan, "A Fat Baby Today Means a Patient Tomorrow."

Some prepared food issued at hospitals and by baby doctors has been found to upset a baby. It is a powdered mess one is supposed to dissolve in water and feed to the baby.

If you ever tasted it, you would agree with the baby. It's terrible.

More than that, it is total carbohydrate and does not contain the protein necessary to make tissue and bone. It only makes fat. When you see one of these bloated, modern babies, know that it is being fed exactly on a diet of mixed milk powder, glucose and water, total carbohydrate.

The largest cause of upset in a baby's early life is just rations. The baby might be fed, yes. But with what? Terrible tasting, high-carbohydrate powdered milk solutions, or skim breast milk from an overworked mother. A ration *must* contain a heavy percentage of *protein*. Protein is the building block for nerves and bones. A soldier, wounded, will not heal without heavy protein intake. Ulcers will not get well without a heavy protein diet being given.

To make brain, bone and tissue, the baby *must* be given protein. And from two days old to at least three years. That makes strong, pretty, alert babies that sleep well and do well.

This problem was first tackled as a personal matter. As a father with a little boy who was not going to live, fast action had to be taken to save him. He had to be (1) gotten *out* of the hospital and (2) the trouble discovered and (3) remedied. The total time available was less than twenty-four hours. He was dying.

So (1) he was gotten out of the hospital. And (2) it was found he wouldn't or couldn't eat. And (3) a formula that provided him the nutrition he needed was developed and given to him.

The formula utilized barley. Roman troops had marched while living on a diet of barley, the cereal with the highest protein content. This formula is the nearest approach to human milk that can be assembled easily. It is an old Roman formula, no less, from around 2,200 years ago.

It's a bit of trouble, of course. You have to sacrifice a pot or a small kettle to cook the barley in (it really wrecks a pot, so you just have a barley pot and use only it). And you have to cook barley for a long time to get barley water, and you may forget and it burns. But even so, it's worth it in terms of a calmer house and a healthy baby.

You mix up a full twenty-four-hour batch of this barley recipe every day, bottle it in sterilized bottles and put it where it will remain cold. And you heat a bottle up to 98.6° F or thereabouts (test it by squirting some on the back of the hand to see if it's too warm or too cool) before you give it to the baby.

And, although you *try* to keep the baby on a schedule, you are foolish not to feed him or her when the baby is hungry.

A baby, having eaten a full ration, usually sleeps for hours anyway. If they don't, there is always a reason, such as a pin or a piece of coal in the bed, wet diapers, something. When a baby who shouldn't be crying, does, hunt until you find out why. Don't follow the schools of (1) the baby is just willful or (2) it's a serious illness that requires an immediate operation. Somewhere between we find the real reason.

Barley Formula for Babies

The foremost reason a baby doesn't do well is poor rations. And to remedy that, here is a formula one can use:

15 ounces of barley water

10 ounces of homogenized milk

3 ounces of corn syrup

The amount of syrup should be varied—depending on the baby—some like it weak—some take it stronger.

This formula can be multiplied by any number according to the number of bottles desired but the ratio remains the same.

To make the barley water, put about half a cup of *whole barley* in a piece of muslin, tie loosely to allow for expansion. It is *slowly* boiled in a covered, vented pot not made of aluminum for 6½ hours in about 4 pints of water. (In venting the pot, one allows steam to escape either through a vent built in the lid [if there is one] or by placing the cover slightly askew so there is an opening between the cover and pot.) Barley water will turn very, very pink. This gives about the right consistency of barley water for making the formula as above.

You don't feed the baby the actual barley, only the water mixed with the milk and corn syrup, in the ratio as given in the formula above.

Do not add anything else to this formula, such as vitamins or cream "to make the formula more nutritious." The formula is as laid out above.

Use this formula and have healthier babies!

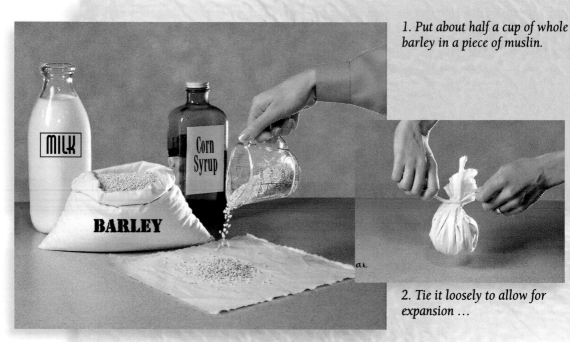

1. Put about half a cup of whole barley in a piece of muslin.

2. Tie it loosely to allow for expansion ...

3. ... and place it in the pot containing 4 pints of water.

4. Boil slowly for 6½ hours with pot slightly vented so steam can escape.

6 ½ hours

5. Mix the formula using a ratio of: 15 ounces of barley water, 10 ounces of homogenized milk, 3 ounces of corn syrup.

10 OZ.

3 OZ.

15 OZ.

HOMOGENIZED MILK

CORN SYRUP

BARLEY WATER

6. Keep the formula cold until feeding time.

98.6°F

7. Heat a bottle to 98.6° F (body temperature).

8. Squirt a few drops on your hand to ensure neither too hot nor too cold. Then give it to the baby.

BARLEY FORMULA

Put about half a cup of whole barley in a piece of muslin.

Tie loosely.

Boil slowly for 6½ hours in about 4 pints of water.

Mix the formula in a ratio of:

      15 ounces of barley water

      10 ounces of homogenized milk

      3 ounces of corn syrup

CREATING TOMORROW'S SOCIETY

Working with children can be a fascinating adventure. The person who applies insight and patience along with his skill in applying the knowledge and techniques laid out in this booklet will be rewarded by seeing children progress to become cooperative, healthy members of the society. The task may seem impossible and heartbreaking at times, but in the end there will be an unequaled sense of accomplishment, of having done something really worthwhile for the advancement of future generations.■

PRACTICAL EXERCISES

The following exercises will help you understand this booklet and increase your ability to deal with children better.

1 Observe someone handling a child. Notice if the person tries persuasion or force to get a child to do something against his will. If so, what were the results and how would the materials of this booklet have been applied instead? Then observe someone else handling a child and do the same as you did in the first example.

2 Write down an example of how a child can contribute to you. Describe the circumstances you would encounter and what you would do to allow the child to contribute in that circumstance. Then, do this again— thinking of another example of how a child could contribute to you and how you would handle the circumstance.

3 Applying the material in this booklet, consult a child's willingness and get him to do something you need or want him to do.

4 Using the data you read in this booklet, locate and handle a child who has hurt himself and does not spontaneously recover. Ensure you apply the data about saying nothing when the child is hurt. Carry out the steps to handle the child until he gets bored or laughs.

5 Handle a child who is crying until he stops crying. Apply the data in the section, "Tell Me About It," having the child relay his story in present time if he doesn't do this spontaneously. Carry out the steps to handle the crying child until he gets bored or laughs.

6 Write down five examples of actions a parent could do or things he could say which would direct a child's attention and keep him safe without using constant verbal restraints.

7 Improve a child's memory by having him tell you past pleasure moments. Use the techniques found in the booklet section, "Handling a Child's Upsets and Mishaps" to accomplish this result.

RESULTS FROM APPLICATION

It isn't easy to raise children well in today's busy and pressured society. The demands of work and finances, the high divorce rate, the availability of drugs in our schools, the failing educational system all contribute to an unstable family environment. It isn't easy for parents or for their children.

Yet the technology of how to raise happy children does exist. And it has been used by thousands of parents and others to change lives.

All of the Scientology principles which apply to adults also apply to children, but there is also an entire body of work that specifically addresses these men and women who have not "attained full growth." By using this wisdom, raising children can be a joyful and rewarding experience.

The examples below demonstrate that people can indeed bring up children who are able to survive and be happy in this sometimes confusing world.

A woman married a man who had three children. Her sister saw that she was mishandling these children in much the same way as she had been mishandled as a child.

"I had just learned some of Mr. Hubbard's discoveries of how the mind works and how mishandling children can be handed down from one generation to

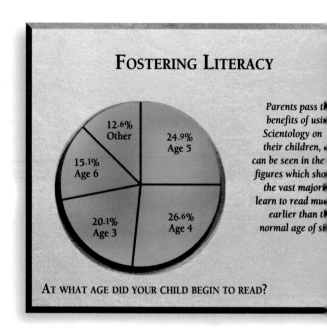

FOSTERING LITERACY

- 12.6% Other
- 24.9% Age 5
- 15.1% Age 6
- 20.1% Age 3
- 26.6% Age 4

Parents pass t
benefits of usi
Scientology on
their children,
can be seen in the
figures which sho
the vast majori
learn to read mu
earlier than t
normal age of si

AT WHAT AGE DID YOUR CHILD BEGIN TO READ?

the next. So with these basics, I sat my sister down and went over with her how she had been ignored and mistreated as a child, to which she agreed. I also got her to see that she was very able and naturally wanted to do the correct thing, even when she was a small child. I asked her how she would have responded if someone had actually communicated with her when she was a child and also got her to look at how she could do this with her stepchildren and she brightened up a lot. After that my sister, who had previously not liked or wanted children, changed dramatically. She started enjoying the children, and also decided to have one of her own. Since this time she allows her children to communicate to her and be the individuals they are. She loves being a mother now and I believe that this has made her life much happier, not to mention the lives of her children."

Applying L. Ron Hubbard's data about handling small children to the life of a young boy, a nanny brought about a remarkable change:

"The little boy loved being at school, but on the way home each day would fight with his brothers in the car, yelling and fussing about where to sit and so forth. This would continue at the dinner table, where he was really unpleasant to be around and would upset the rest of the family. His parents didn't know what to do to handle him except to send him to his room. This only resulted in the yelling coming from the room until he tired out. I applied the datum that in such circumstances there is a specific thing wrong and one must hunt to find out what it is. I found out that since he had started school, he had no longer been taking naps in the afternoon and he was exhausted at the end of the day. So I moved his bedtime to earlier and in a matter of days he was a most charming, lovable five-year-old boy who eagerly talked about what he did at school and said, 'Please pass the salt' with a smile at the dinner table. To his parents this was a miracle. I made a good impression, but really it was just applying L. Ron Hubbard's technology."

A mother living in Auckland, New Zealand, was quite frantic about her first baby as he cried every few hours, day and night. The family doctor said the child was in good health and could not account for the crying.

"One day I was in our local Scientology church and picked up an article by L. Ron Hubbard about how to have healthy babies. One of his recommendations was to feed a baby with a barley formula which was given in the article. I went home determined to try it out. The results were very worthwhile. In two days my son had settled down to sleeping between feeding times. At the end of a week he began sleeping through his night feeding time. I was so thankful for the extra rest! I later discovered he was cutting teeth—he cut all of them without crying. Diaper rash and upset stomachs were unknowns in our home and he grew so strong that he began walking at seven months. I can honestly say that the barley formula not only had a calming effect on our son but upon the whole household, as I went on to feed our other two children the same way."

Having studied what L. Ron Hubbard wrote about raising children, a father in Los Angeles decided to use this data in the raising of his son. He said:

"I felt I owed my child a parent who didn't pass on the 'family traditions'—bad habits of child raising. I knew I would fall into the rut of a parent with not enough understanding if I didn't do something about it. So I studied L. Ron Hubbard's data so that I could give my son a proper upbringing. The difference that it made, which is observable not only to me but to other parents, is that my son has a real interest in keeping his possessions in order and cared for and he often comments on other people (adults as well) who don't. My wife and I have never required that he be concerned about these things. The secret of accomplishing this lies in applying the data and is actually what you don't understand, not what your child doesn't understand. You would be remiss in your duties as a parent if you didn't read and use this technology."

GLOSSARY

aberration: a departure from rational thought or behavior; irrational thought or conduct. It means basically to err, to make mistakes, or more specifically to have fixed ideas which are not true. The word is also used in its scientific sense. It means departure from a straight line. If a line should go from A to B, then if it is *aberrated* it would go from A to some other point, to some other point, to some other point, to some other point, to some other point, and finally arrive at B. Taken in this sense, it would also mean the lack of straightness or to see crookedly as, for example, a man sees a horse but thinks he sees an elephant. Aberrated conduct would be wrong conduct, or conduct not supported by reason. *Aberration* is opposed to sanity, which would be its opposite. From the Latin, *aberrare*, to wander from; Latin, *ab*, away, *errare*, to wander.

assist: a process which can be done to alleviate a present time discomfort and help a person recover more rapidly from an accident, illness or upset.

communication: an interchange of ideas across space between two individuals.

confront: to face without flinching or avoiding. The ability to confront is actually the ability to be there comfortably and perceive.

Dianetics: comes from the Greek words *dia*, meaning "through" and *nous*, meaning "soul." Dianetics is a methodology developed by L. Ron Hubbard which can help alleviate such ailments as unwanted sensations and emotions, irrational fears and psychosomatic illnesses. It is most accurately described as *what the soul is doing to the body through the mind.*

havingness: the feeling that one owns or possesses; it can also be described as the concept of being able to reach or not being prevented from reaching.

present time: the time which is now and becomes the past as rapidly as it is observed. It is a term loosely applied to the environment existing in now.

reality: that which appears to be. Reality is fundamentally agreement; the degree of agreement reached by people. What we agree to be real is real.

restimulation: the reactivation of a memory of a past unpleasant experience due to similar circumstances in the present approximating circumstances of the past.

Scientology: an applied religious philosophy developed by L. Ron Hubbard. It is the study and handling of the spirit in relationship to itself, universes and other life. The word *Scientology* comes from the Latin *scio*, which means "know" and the Greek word *logos*, meaning "the word or outward form by which the inward thought is expressed and made known." Thus, Scientology means knowing about knowing.

self-determinism: that state of being wherein the individual can or cannot be controlled by his environment according to his own choice. In that state the individual has self-confidence in his control of the material universe and other people.

ABOUT L. RON HUBBARD

Born in Tilden, Nebraska on March 13, 1911, his road of discovery and dedication to his fellows began at an early age. By the age of nineteen, he had traveled more than a quarter of a million miles, examining the cultures of Java, Japan, India and the Philippines.

Returning to the United States in 1929, Ron resumed his formal education and studied mathematics, engineering and the then new field of nuclear physics—all providing vital tools for continued research. To finance that research, Ron embarked upon a literary career in the early 1930s, and soon became one of the most widely read authors of popular fiction. Yet never losing sight of his primary goal, he continued his mainline research through extensive travel and expeditions.

With the advent of World War II, he entered the United States Navy as a lieutenant (junior grade) and served as commander of antisubmarine corvettes. Left partially blind and lame from injuries sustained during combat, he was diagnosed as permanently disabled by 1945. Through application of his theories on the mind, however, he was not only able to help fellow servicemen, but also to regain his own health.

After five more years of intensive research, Ron's discoveries were presented to the world in *Dianetics: The Modern Science of Mental Health.* The first popular handbook on the human mind expressly written for the man in the street, *Dianetics* ushered in a new era of hope for mankind and a new phase of life for its author. He did, however, not cease his research, and as breakthrough after breakthrough was carefully codified through late 1951, the applied religious philosophy of Scientology was born.

Because Scientology explains the whole of life, there is no aspect of man's existence that L. Ron Hubbard's subsequent work did not address. Residing variously in the United States and England, his continued research brought forth solutions to such social ills as declining educational standards and pandemic drug abuse.

All told, L. Ron Hubbard's works on Scientology and Dianetics total forty million words of recorded lectures, books and writings. Together, these constitute the legacy of a lifetime that ended on January 24, 1986. Yet the passing of L. Ron Hubbard in no way constituted an end; for with a hundred million of his books in circulation and millions of people daily applying his technologies for betterment, it can truly be said the world still has no greater friend.■

CHURCHES OF SCIENTOLOGY
Contact Your Nearest Church or Organization
or visit www.volunteerministers.org

UNITED STATES

ALBUQUERQUE
Church of Scientology
8106 Menaul Boulevard NE
Albuquerque, New Mexico
87110

ANN ARBOR
Church of Scientology
66 E. Michigan Avenue
Battle Creek, Michigan 49017

ATLANTA
Church of Scientology
1611 Mt. Vernon Road
Dunwoody, Georgia 30338

AUSTIN
Church of Scientology
2200 Guadalupe
Austin, Texas 78705

BOSTON
Church of Scientology
448 Beacon Street
Boston, Massachusetts 02115

BUFFALO
Church of Scientology
47 West Huron Street
Buffalo, New York 14202

CHICAGO
Church of Scientology
3011 North Lincoln Avenue
Chicago, Illinois 60657-4207

CINCINNATI
Church of Scientology
215 West 4th Street, 5th Floor
Cincinnati, Ohio 45202-2670

CLEARWATER
Church of Scientology
Flag Service Organization
210 South Fort Harrison Avenue
Clearwater, Florida 33756

Foundation Church of
Scientology
Flag Ship Service Organization
c/o Freewinds Relay Office
118 North Fort Harrison Avenue
Clearwater, Florida 33755-4013

COLUMBUS
Church of Scientology
30 North High Street
Columbus, Ohio 43215

DALLAS
Church of Scientology
Celebrity Centre Dallas
1850 North Buckner Boulevard
Dallas, Texas 75228

DENVER
Church of Scientology
3385 South Bannock Street
Englewood, Colorado 80110

DETROIT
Church of Scientology
28000 Middlebelt Road
Farmington Hills, Michigan
48334

HONOLULU
Church of Scientology
1146 Bethel Street
Honolulu, Hawaii 96813

KANSAS CITY
Church of Scientology
3619 Broadway
Kansas City, Missouri 64111

LAS VEGAS
Church of Scientology
846 East Sahara Avenue
Las Vegas, Nevada 89104

Church of Scientology
Celebrity Centre Las Vegas
4850 W. Flamingo Road, Suite 10
Las Vegas, Nevada 89103

LONG ISLAND
Church of Scientology
99 Railroad Station Plaza
Hicksville, New York
11801-2850

LOS ANGELES AND VICINITY
Church of Scientology
of Los Angeles
4810 Sunset Boulevard
Los Angeles, California 90027

Church of Scientology
1451 Irvine Boulevard
Tustin, California 92680

Church of Scientology
1277 East Colorado Boulevard
Pasadena, California 91106

Church of Scientology
15643 Sherman Way
Van Nuys, California 91406

Church of Scientology
American Saint Hill
Organization
1413 L. Ron Hubbard Way
Los Angeles, California 90027

Church of Scientology
American Saint Hill Foundation
1413 L. Ron Hubbard Way
Los Angeles, California 90027

Church of Scientology
Advanced Organization
of Los Angeles
1306 L. Ron Hubbard Way
Los Angeles, California 90027

Church of Scientology
Celebrity Centre International
5930 Franklin Avenue
Hollywood, California 90028

LOS GATOS
Church of Scientology
2155 South Bascom Avenue,
Suite 120
Campbell, California 95008

MIAMI
Church of Scientology
120 Giralda Avenue
Coral Gables, Florida 33134

MINNEAPOLIS
Church of Scientology
Twin Cities
1011 Nicollet Mall
Minneapolis, Minnesota 55403

MOUNTAIN VIEW
Church of Scientology
2483 Old Middlefield Way
Mountain View, California
94043

NASHVILLE
Church of Scientology
Celebrity Centre Nashville
1204 16th Avenue South
Nashville, Tennessee 37212

NEW HAVEN
Church of Scientology
909 Whalley Avenue
New Haven, Connecticut
06515-1728

NEW YORK CITY
Church of Scientology
227 West 46th Street
New York, New York
10036-1409

Church of Scientology
Celebrity Centre New York
65 East 82nd Street
New York, New York 10028

ORLANDO
Church of Scientology
1830 East Colonial Drive
Orlando, Florida 32803-4729

PHILADELPHIA
Church of Scientology
1315 Race Street
Philadelphia, Pennsylvania
19107

PHOENIX
Church of Scientology
2111 West University Drive
Mesa, Arizona 85201

PORTLAND
Church of Scientology
2636 NE Sandy Boulevard
Portland, Oregon 97232-2342

Church of Scientology
Celebrity Centre Portland
708 SW Salmon Street
Portland, Oregon 97205

SACRAMENTO
Church of Scientology
825 15th Street
Sacramento, California
95814-2096

SALT LAKE CITY
Church of Scientology
1931 South 1100 East
Salt Lake City, Utah 84106

SAN DIEGO
Church of Scientology
1330 4th Avenue
San Diego, California 92101

SAN FRANCISCO
Church of Scientology
83 McAllister Street
San Francisco, California 94102

SAN JOSE
Church of Scientology
80 East Rosemary Street
San Jose, California 95112

SANTA BARBARA
Church of Scientology
524 State Street
Santa Barbara, California 93101

SEATTLE
Church of Scientology
2226 3rd Avenue
Seattle, Washington 98121

ST. LOUIS
Church of Scientology
6901 Delmar Boulevard
University City, Missouri 63130

TAMPA
Church of Scientology
3102 N. Havana Avenue
Tampa, Florida 33607

WASHINGTON, DC
Founding Church of Scientology
of Washington, DC
1701 20th Street NW
Washington, DC 20009

PUERTO RICO

HATO REY
Dianetics Center of Puerto Rico
272 JT Piñero Avenue
Hyde Park
San Juan, Puerto Rico 00918

CANADA

EDMONTON
Church of Scientology
10206 106th Street NW
Edmonton, Alberta
Canada T5J 1H7

KITCHENER
Church of Scientology
104 King Street West, 2nd Floor
Kitchener, Ontario
Canada N2G 1A6

MONTREAL
Church of Scientology
4489 Papineau Street
Montreal, Quebec
Canada H2H 1T7

OTTAWA
Church of Scientology
150 Rideau Street, 2nd Floor
Ottawa, Ontario
Canada K1N 5X6

QUEBEC
Church of Scientology
350 Bd Chareste Est
Quebec, Quebec
Canada G1K 3H5

TORONTO
Church of Scientology
696 Yonge Street, 2nd Floor
Toronto, Ontario
Canada M4Y 2A7

VANCOUVER
Church of Scientology
401 West Hastings Street
Vancouver, British Columbia
Canada V6B 1L5

WINNIPEG
Church of Scientology
315 Garry Street, Suite 210
Winnipeg, Manitoba
Canada R3B 2G7

UNITED KINGDOM

BIRMINGHAM
Church of Scientology
8 Ethel Street
Winston Churchill House
Birmingham, England B2 4BG

BRIGHTON
Church of Scientology
Third Floor, 79-83 North Street
Brighton, Sussex
England BN1 1ZA

EAST GRINSTEAD
Church of Scientology
Saint Hill Foundation
Saint Hill Manor
East Grinstead, West Sussex
England RH19 4JY

Advanced Organization
  Saint Hill
Saint Hill Manor
East Grinstead, West Sussex
England RH19 4JY

EDINBURGH
Hubbard Academy of Personal
  Independence
20 Southbridge
Edinburgh, Scotland EH1 1LL

LONDON
Church of Scientology
68 Tottenham Court Road
London, England W1P 0BB

Church of Scientology
Celebrity Centre London
42 Leinster Gardens
London, England W2 3AN

MANCHESTER
Church of Scientology
258 Deansgate
Manchester, England M3 4BG

PLYMOUTH
Church of Scientology
41 Ebrington Street
Plymouth, Devon
England PL4 9AA

SUNDERLAND
Church of Scientology
51 Fawcett Street
Sunderland, Tyne and Wear
England SR1 1RS

AUSTRALIA

ADELAIDE
Church of Scientology
24-28 Waymouth Street
Adelaide, South Australia
Australia 5000

BRISBANE
Church of Scientology
106 Edward Street, 2nd Floor
Brisbane, Queensland
Australia 4000

CANBERRA
Church of Scientology
43-45 East Row
Canberra City, ACT
Australia 2601

MELBOURNE
Church of Scientology
42-44 Russell Street
Melbourne, Victoria
Australia 3000

PERTH
Church of Scientology
108 Murray Street, 1st Floor
Perth, Western Australia
Australia 6000

SYDNEY
Church of Scientology
201 Castlereagh Street
Sydney, New South Wales
Australia 2000

Church of Scientology
Advanced Organization
  Saint Hill Australia,
  New Zealand and Oceania
19-37 Greek Street
Glebe, New South Wales
Australia 2037

NEW ZEALAND

AUCKLAND
Church of Scientology
159 Queen Street, 3rd Floor
Auckland 1, New Zealand

AFRICA

BULAWAYO
Church of Scientology
Southampton House, Suite 202
Main Street and 9th Avenue
Bulawayo, Zimbabwe

CAPE TOWN
Church of Scientology
Ground Floor, Dorlane House
39 Roeland Street
Cape Town 8001, South Africa

DURBAN
Church of Scientology
20 Buckingham Terrace
Westville, Durban 3630
South Africa

HARARE
Church of Scientology
404-409 Pockets Building
50 Jason Moyo Avenue
Harare, Zimbabwe

JOHANNESBURG
Church of Scientology
4th Floor, Budget House
130 Main Street
Johannesburg 2001
South Africa

Church of Scientology
No. 108 1st Floor,
  Bordeaux Centre
Gordon Road, Corner Jan
  Smuts Avenue
Blairgowrie, Randburg 2125
South Africa

PORT ELIZABETH
Church of Scientology
2 St. Christopher's
27 Westbourne Road Central
Port Elizabeth 6001
South Africa

PRETORIA
Church of Scientology
307 Ancore Building
Corner Jeppe and Esselen Streets
Sunnyside, Pretoria 0002
South Africa

SCIENTOLOGY MISSIONS

INTERNATIONAL OFFICE
Scientology Missions
  International
6331 Hollywood Boulevard
  Suite 501
Los Angeles, California
90028-6314

UNITED STATES
Scientology Missions
  International
Western United States Office
1308 L. Ron Hubbard Way
Los Angeles, California 90027

Scientology Missions
  International
Eastern United States Office
349 W. 48th Street
New York, New York 10036

Scientology Missions
  International
Flag Land Base Office
210 South Fort Harrison Avenue
Clearwater, Florida 33756

AFRICA
Scientology Missions
  International
African Office
6th Floor, Budget House
130 Main Street
Johannesburg 2001
South Africa

AUSTRALIA, NEW ZEALAND AND OCEANIA
Scientology Missions
  International
Australian, New Zealand
  and Oceanian Office
201 Castlereagh Street, 3rd Flr.
Sydney, New South Wales
Australia 2000

CANADA
Scientology Missions
  International
Canadian Office
696 Yonge Street
Toronto, Ontario
Canada M4Y 2A7

UNITED KINGDOM
Scientology Missions
  International
United Kingdom Office
Saint Hill Manor
East Grinstead, West Sussex,
England RH19 4JY

TO OBTAIN ANY BOOKS OR CAS-
SETTES BY L. RON HUBBARD WHICH
ARE NOT AVAILABLE AT YOUR LOCAL
ORGANIZATION, CONTACT ANY OF
THE FOLLOWING PUBLICATIONS
ORGANIZATIONS WORLDWIDE:

BRIDGE PUBLICATIONS, INC.
4751 Fountain Avenue
Los Angeles, California 90029
www.bridgepub.com

NEW ERA PUBLICATIONS
INTERNATIONAL ApS
Store Kongensgade 53
1264 Copenhagen K
Denmark
www.newerapublications.com

BUILD A BETTER WORLD

BECOME A VOLUNTEER MINISTER

Help bring happiness, purpose and truth to your fellow man.
Become a Volunteer Minister.

Thousands of Volunteer Ministers bring relief and sanity to others all over the world using techniques like the ones found in this booklet. But more help is needed. Your help.
As a Volunteer Minister you can today handle things which seemed impossible yesterday. And you can vastly improve this world's tomorrow.
Become a Volunteer Minister and brighten the world to a better place for you to live.
It's easy to do. For help and information about becoming a Volunteer Minister, visit our website today. www.volunteerministers.org
You can also call or write your nearest Volunteer Ministers International organization.

VOLUNTEER MINISTERS INTERNATIONAL
A DEPARTMENT OF THE INTERNATIONAL HUBBARD ECCLESIASTICAL LEAGUE OF PASTORS

INTERNATIONAL OFFICE
6331 Hollywood Boulevard, Suite 708
Los Angeles, California 90028
Tel: (323) 960-3560 (800) 435-7498

WESTERN US
1308 L. Ron Hubbard Way
Los Angeles, California 90027
Tel: (323) 953-3357
1-888-443-5760
ihelpwestus@earthlink.net

EASTERN US
349 W. 48th Street
New York, New York 10036
Tel: (212) 757-9610
1-888-443-5788

CANADA
696 Yonge Street
Toronto, Ontario
Canada M4Y 2A7
Tel: (416) 968-0070

LATIN AMERICA
Federación Mexicana de
 Dianética, A.C.
Puebla #31
Colonia Roma, CP 06700
Mexico, D.F.
Tel: 525-511-4452

EUROPE
Store Kongensgade 55
1264 Copenhagen K
Denmark
Tel: 45-33-737-322

ITALY
Via Cadorna, 61
20090 Vimodrone (MI)
Italy
Tel: 39-0227-409-246

AUSTRALIA
201 Castlereagh Street
3rd Floor
Sydney, New South Wales
Australia 2000
Tel: 612-9267-6422

AFRICA
6th Floor, Budget House
130 Main Street
Johannesburg 2001
South Africa
Tel: 083-331-7170

UNITED KINGDOM
Saint Hill Manor
East Grinstead, West Sussex
England RH19 4JY
Tel: 44-1342-301-895

HUNGARY
1438 Budapest
PO Box 351, Hungary
Tel: 361-321-5298

COMMONWEALTH OF INDEPENDENT STATES
c/o Hubbard Humanitarian
 Center
Ul. Borisa Galushkina 19A
129301 Moscow, Russia
Tel: 7-095-961-3414

TAIWAN
2F, 65, Sec. 4
Ming-Sheng East Road
Taipei, Taiwan ROC
Tel: 88-628-770-5074

www.volunteerministers.org

Bridge Publications, Inc.
4751 Fountain Avenue, Los Angeles, CA 90029

ISBN 0-88404-921-3

©1994, 2001 L. Ron Hubbard Library. All Rights Reserved. Any unauthorized copying, translation, duplication, importation or distribution, in whole or in part, by any means, including electronic copying, storage or transmission, is a violation of applicable laws.

Scientology, Dianetics, Celebrity Centre, L. Ron Hubbard, Flag, the L. Ron Hubbard Signature, the Scientology Cross (rounded) and the Scientology Cross (pointed) are trademarks and service marks owned by Religious Technology Center and are used with its permission.

NEW ERA is a trademark and service mark.

Bridge Publications, Inc. is a registered trademark and service mark in California and it is owned by Bridge Publications, Inc.

Printed in Colombia

An L. RON HUBBARD Publication